TheLIST

3.   ANALIST

7.   VISUALIST

13.   REALIST

17.   FINALIST

So, this particular night I'm at home minding

my own business when my phone rings.

A close friend of mine calls to vent and as always

I lent my listening ear.

She starts rambling on how she is tired of dating and
not finding what she wants, so I asked her

WHAT DO YOU WANT?

so she gets started,

" I want a guy who...

is a man of God   **has 800 credit score**

got a six pack   **has flawless hands**

&

The List goes on and on...

She finally ended her rant like,

"I Just don't know what the issue is?"

So me being me, as real as they come,

this is the answer I gave her;

The Issue is You

Yes, You

That's Right

I'm talking to you reading these words

YOU ARE THE ISSUE!

But luckily there's a solution to the issue;

First be honest with yourself.

This is where the initial list comes in.

It's where you analyze

who you are

and what you are,

hence the name...

ANA-LIST

This is the time you get to be full of yourself.

Come on sing-a-long with me

"I'm Feeling Myself, Feeling Myself"

as you write this List, LOL

_____	_____
_____	_____
_____	_____
_____	_____
_____	_____
_____	_____
_____	_____
_____	_____
_____	_____
_____	_____

_____

_____

_____

_____

_____

_____

_____

_____

_____

_____

Ok, now that you have a list of what you can offer an individual,

lets get into

WHAT YOU WANT!

Here you will write down all the things you want in your

PERFECT MATE

and I mean

EVERYTHING!

Leave Nothing Out!

Write down every desire, hope, want & need.

I know we all have had this picture in our mind for the longest time

but actually seeing the complete list

before your eyes will make it

simple & possible.

This is the reason it is called the...

VISUA-LIST

It's a visualized blueprint of the ideal mate!

You can be specific and as picky as you want. So if you "like big butts and cannot lie"

then write it down, LOL

_____ _____

_____ _____

_____ _____

_____ _____

_____ _____

_____ _____

_____ _____

_____ _____

_____ _____

_____ _____

_____

_____

_____

_____

_____

_____

_____

_____

_____

_____

Now that you have the perfect list, it's time for the REAL work to begin to get you this mate you desire.

Begin by asking yourself this:

Now that I have my ideal mate in mind,

Am I the ideal mate they have in mind?

You may be asking yourself:

How would I know?

Well this is the part where you become

REALISTIC

Your list although,

Perfect to You

is not

Perfect for You

What I mean by that is BE REAL WITH YOURSELF

Please, don't be like my friend, wanting a man of God but not even trying to become a

Woman of God.

Like, lets be honest,

You can't tell Psalms from Proverbs

but you want a deacon, LOL

My point is…

Are the things you wrote on your VISUA-LIST,
things you are, have, have been doing, becoming or
willing to do?

(Go Check Your List)

If any of it you said NO to,

then it shouldn't be on your list

TAKE IT OFF!

However if you said YES,

then you are on track to getting all you ever wanted!
Quick question,

Do you see any of the things from your

ANA-LIST on the VISUA-LIST?

Well, You Should!

I mean you should be seeing apart of yourself in the
person you want, duh!

So now that you crossed those things off of your
VISUA-LIST

You did cross them off, right?

REA-LIST

Then it's time to write down your new list here

The Realistic one that is!

This List should reflect just that,

so get to writing...

_____   _____

_____   _____

_____   _____

_____   _____

_____   _____

_____   _____

_____   _____

_____   _____

_____   _____

_____   _____

_____

_____

_____

_____

_____

_____

_____

_____

_____

_____

So now I need you to reflect on the REA-LIST and determine how you are going to become these things on The List.

For example, if a six pack is on your list, like my friend who has nothing but one full pack in sight, LOL

Then I suggest an active approach would be formulating a home workout plan.

Like I told her, You have to do a burpee or something, smh

But seriously this helps you to get started on achieving your six pack you are desiring

Maybe even consider getting a gym membership,

I mean you never know

You just may meet someone there, OK!

and at that point you will need

"THE RULE BOOK"

Hello!

The next list is the list where you write your plan on achieving the things on your REA-LIST

This is literally the Final Step in the process of getting and having

"THE ONE"

It's the very reason it is called the...

FINA-LIST

Write down all the things you have to do to get what you want,

Be sure to list it in full & final detail!

_____	_____
_____	_____
_____	_____
_____	_____
_____	_____
_____	_____
_____	_____
_____	_____
_____	_____
_____	_____

_____

_____

_____

_____

_____

_____

_____

_____

_____

_____

So now that you have done the work,

here are some GEMS to note……

If you are currently in a relationship,

this book will help you to identify if you are living up to their expectations and if they are living up to yours

You just may find out:

That you have been settling or

not that interested in your current situation as much or on the other hand

It can help you to identify issues you have in your current situation and help to correct them.

I mean come on people,

we ain't getting any younger

&

As for you singles,

this book will help you not to waste your time with someone whom you know you would not date,

"Cuz ain't nobody got time for that!"

and NEVER forget...

You'll

Find

The One

When you

Become

The One

Follow The Author:

@JPWritesPub

&

Complete your EVOL series with the following books:

Find them on Amazon in print as well as Kindle!

This book is brought to you by:

J.P. WRITES

PUBLISHING

Cover done by @TheArtisician

Made in the USA
Columbia, SC
12 March 2021